BECOMING A BETTER ME: A 45 DAY MOTIVATIONAL JOURNAL

BECOMING A BETTER ME: A 45 DAY MOTIVATIONAL JOURNAL

◆ ◆ ◆

Terrelle Smith

ISBN: 161133960X
ISBN 13: 9781611339604

Terrelle Smith is a sort after Motivational Speaker, not only has she spoken at women conferences, she has also spoken to book clubs as well as various women groups across the United States. Terrelle believes that no group is too small for empowerment. Going through many trials in her life, she decided to allow God to use those trials as a launching pad to encourage women of all ages become a better person by doing a self examination.

"God loves us so much that he fearfully and wonderfully made us" psalm 139:14 (Back Cover of book)

For I know the thoughts that I think toward you, saith the LORD, thoughts of peace, and not of evil, to give you an expected end. Then shall ye call upon me, and ye shall go and pray unto me, and I will hearken unto you. Jeremiah 29:11-12

So many times people mistake the anointing on your life as being a bold, overly confident female. As a matter of fact, the person that has the anointing sometimes has a fear of asserting themselves because of the criticism or rejection they know they will receive. Being rejected or criticized by former friends and ever present family members is hard to absorb. Nothing you do will please them because you have come out from among them, as God has instructed.

Throughout the Bible we see that God selects whom he chooses to perform his work and most of them have been ordinary in their approaches to life. Some have tried to run and hide, pretending that they were not called or did not hear God's voice. Never the less, they had gifts, and what they were lacking, God provided. This is nothing new, as the account of Queen Esther shows in the Old Testament. Once she accepted God's calling on her life she had to come to the realization that if she perished, she perished. This called for strong faith. When I look at people like Harriet Tubman risking her life so others could be free or Rosa Parks taking a stand to change the status quo that resulted in African Americans being able to ride a bus and sit in any seat lets me know that if God is for you, who can be against you. Women of all races have struggled with accepting the challenges of the calling on their lives. I had to realize that there are blessings and burdens that comes with the divinely chosen.

When God does a work in you, it is hard to contain it. He said that you would be a new person, old things are passed away, behold all things are new. I'm sure that most of you that are reading this are dealing with the same thing, I know I am! This dates back centuries ago when the slaves were in existence and even men positions as Kings felt threatened by assertive women. But let's be honest, we have sometimes been our own worst enemy. We as women, were always put in a position to fight or shall I say compete against one another. Even now when we see strong women leaders walking in their gift instead of lifting them up, we immediately look for anything negative. I sometimes think many slaves stayed in bondage because in their minds, they were still in bondage. I strongly feel that many females never got free because of their own struggles of not knowing when or whom to follow. It is proven this is still going on in society today because too many of us want to be in a leadership role without first learning how to follow! Jesus led us, but he also was a servant too. Today there are so many women in dual roles. Being the mother and the father to their kids, it is sometimes hard to turn off the dominant role outside of the home because many women have become a master at it. There is a problem with this because God did not call the women to be the head of the house. God called the man to be the head of the house like he is the head of the church (Ephesians 5:23).

Many mothers have taught their daughters to be this "Independent" woman that depends on no one. There is a problem with that; we have stopped following God's divine order. God said in his word that there is power in unity! We have to connect with other sisters in Christ. We need each other!

Being raised in a household that had a mother that was very goal oriented, taught me how to be a diligent worker. Seeing her like a superwoman when it came to her kids was an everyday norm to me and my siblings. This was a memory that would last me a lifetime and that I would pass on to my child. Many of you reading this did not have a role model present in your life to pass on certain positive morals. The great news is that Jesus is your role model. He is the example of Positivity at its best!

My Dad was also present but he played a pivotal role in my life in another aspect. He was more of the security for the household, the disciplinarian. This caused me to find a mate that would resemble my father.

Even though I had an earthly father, there is nothing like my spiritual father that is in heaven. He can teach us things that no man can. He is the example of what we should look for in a husband here on earth. In many households today, girls are growing up seeing the women carry the dominant role in the house because of the absence of the man. We all know that Jesus was surrounded by women in the Bible during his journey. Seeing my mom work 15 hour days, come home fix dinner, take care of house chores and be the wife to my dad, had to be in only God's strength. Many of you are in this position right now, you barely have time for yourself, and you are raising kids, working a job working two jobs at that! Trying to study for school, taking care of the house, be the perfect wife along with being the women God called you to be.

This is mind boggling and we have to ask God to help us prioritize that which is important to him.

You have so many things going on to where you can't concentrate on spending time with yourself, yet alone God. In order for you to be productive and know what God is calling you to do, you must get in that secret place and spend time consecrating yourself before him and listen to his direction. This is hard for many of us because we do a lot of talking and not enough listening. God wants to use you in the up building of his kingdom but he cannot use you if you're tired, worn down and broken. This is a tactic of the enemy, he wants you to be distracted from your walk, feel tired all the time, feel broken and feel like you don't deserve any of God's blessings. But, we know that God gives salvation and it is free, God paid a high price for your life, he takes pleasure seeing you live your life abundantly in his word.

We all want the blessings of God, but in order to get the blessings of God; we have to put our work in. God has already given us the blueprint of how to survive and how to live this life; we just have to stop long enough to read it. I'm sure if we do read the blueprint, we would get to the goal mine that God has promised in his word. This Christian walk is a lifestyle; it is not to be confused with a gimmick or a scheme. God wants all of you; he doesn't want half of you. 99% of you is still not 100% of you in God's eyes, so we cannot give God some of us and expect all of God's blessing. It is not going to work. As you take a walk through this 45 day devotional/ journey, I pray that it will bless you as it blessed me in preparing it. Take time for yourself to read your devotional daily, write your thoughts in your journal. Go back over your journal and revisit what you have written. (Habakkuk 2:2) Write the vision and make it plain so that you can read through your journey along the way and you can track your progress to see how God has manifested his work in your life.

Take a break throughout the day and meditate on God's word. See the goodness of the Lord in your life. He delights in you and he wants to see you succeed. Walk in wisdom; have a pure and clean heart being transparent so you can be a testimony to others.

God loves you! He gave his son, Jesus, to die for you, that's how much he loves you; so love him just as much as he loves you!

Blessings,

Terrelle

D A Y 1

◆ ◆ ◆

THERE IS POWER in Unity! The enemy wants nothing more than to separate the believers in Christ. There is a spirit of division/hypocrisy in the body of Christ that is causing many to turn their backs on the Church (God). The church is inside of us, that means the anointing is in us that we should carry to the building (the place of worship)! Sadly, not all that worship in the build.

[17]I urge you, brothers, to watch out for those who cause divisions and put obstacles in your way that are contrary to the teaching you have learned. Keep away from them. [18]for such people are not serving our Lord Christ, but their own appetites. By smooth talk and flattery they deceive the minds of naive people. (Romans16:17-18)

In your quiet time, list the things that may be causing division among you and other believers, friends, relationships, family etc...

DAY 2

Don't give the enemy (people being used) power over your thoughts/emotions. Make it on "PURPOSE" to have a great day. The blessing you've been praying for may be right in front of you!

Casting down imaginations, and every high thing that exalteth itself against the knowledge of God, and bringing into captivity every thought to the obedience of Christ; (2Cor.10:5)

List all of the distractions that are hindering you from giving God all of you including your thought life.

D A Y 3

◆ ◆ ◆

WE ARE TO enter God's court with praise. Let's give God a personal praise, not a mechanical praise. Today, take a "praise break" and send up Judah (praise) to the Most High for who he is, not for what he can do.

Enter into his gates with thanksgiving, *and* into his courts with praise: be thankful unto him, *and* bless his name. (Psalm 100:4)

What do you have to praise God for? Think of how God has delivered you from infirmities, bad relationships, and sickness. Etc...

D A Y 4

◆ ◆ ◆

HE MAKES ME to lie down in green pastures and He leads me beside quiet waters.....He is my Jehovah- Shalom: God my peace! Pray to-day about anything that's quieting your peace. Affirm that God is your peace and then pray about God's leading in His work and decisions in your life.

(Psalm 23)

God is a God of peace! Get in a quiet place and have some alone time with him. Write down what he is speaking in your Spirit.

Don't allow the enemy to steal your Joy today. Put on your armor (Ephesians 6) before you leave your house today. Too many times, we allow people to take about what God has freely given to us. Jesus told us to put the armor of God for a reason. This gives us protection against the enemy and his devices. Make sure that you cover your children as well as other believers in Christ.

List things that you need to put under the armor of God.

DAY 6

TODAY IS THE day that the Lord has made, let us rejoice and be glad in it... Take time out to stop and listen. God is speaking to you in that small still voice. That "unction" in your spirit, is the Holy Spirit speaking to you. Let's take time today to talk less and listen more. Get in that secret place where the presence of the Lord is. Your breakthrough is waiting there!

This is the day which the LORD hath made; we will rejoice and be glad in it. (Psalm 118:24)

◆ ◆ ◆

P.U.S.H TODAY (PRAY until something happens) don't give up if it seems like God is silent. He is just exercising your faith. The fervent (without ceasing) prayers of the righteous avail much, so stay before God with consistency. Remember, we must have a clean heart mixed with our faith (hope, confidence). Stay strong, God hears you! It's in God's timing, not ours!

Therefore confess your sins to each other and pray for each other so that you may be healed. The prayer of a righteous man is powerful and effective (James 5:16) NIV

What have you been praying and waiting patiently for?

DAY 8

◆ ◆ ◆

IF GOD IS calling you to do something quit making excuses! Maybe, God has called you to do the impossible in your eyesight. Just know that with every vision, there is provision from God. Sometimes, we just have to launch out into the deep. In Matthew, Jesus told Peter to "come" that is all Jesus said to him. Because of Peter's faith, he stepped out. God is saying "come" step off of the boat of mediocrity. God has called you to greatness. One of my favorite quotes is the one Nike has. "Just do it", something so simple is so powerful! God is waiting on you to "Just do it"! That book, "Just do it", that Ministry, "Just do it"! Whatever it is that you were called to do "Just do it"! God's got your back!!! You are a child of the Most High, you are a King's daughter, the daughter of Zion! Defeat is not in our blood line, because we have the blood of Christ!

(Matthew 14:29)

Can you relate to the Disciple Peter when God told him to step out of the boat? What is keeping you in the boat?

D A Y 9

◆ ◆ ◆

The LORD will perfect that which concerns me;
your mercy, O LORD, endures forever;
do not forsake the works of your hands.

Psalm 138:8

The Lord has called you to greatness! You belong to him so therefore, he wants do a perfect will in you.

What is hindering you from allowing God to do a perfect work in your life?

17

D A Y 1 0

— ◆ ◆ ◆ —

DON'T HESITATE TO lay your plans before the Lord, in fact, it's a must that you do. However, don't be afraid to let God correct your plans. He will give you wisdom if you are willing to receive it and then your plans will become agreeable to His plans for you.

Are your plans lining up with the plans God has for you. If not, ask God for wisdom to come in sync with his plans for you. List some things that you want to line up with God for maximum prosperity.

DAY 11

Take off the spirit of offense today. Put on the armor of God as your defense. You were reined to conquer! You belong to the almighty Jesus Christ! Don't be so easily defeated today; you have the victory over whatever problem or situation that comes your way. Open your mouth and speak thus says the Lord...the word of God and belief is all you need. Quit letting people steal your Joy, if you are then it's just surface Joy and not internal Joy. God said that he came so you may have life and have it more abundantly! So enjoy it!!!!

Are you so easily offended? Think about what offends you and make a list of it.

— ◆ ◆ ◆ —

DON'T BE AFRAID to dance to the music, laugh at a joke, sing a song... it's ok to let go sometimes. Embrace this day, this moment! Love yourself, laugh at yourself, this too is ok! Make it a blessed and best day ever today!

Let your hair down and embrace the freedom you have in Jesus.

List the things that stop you from doing this, and then start declaring authority over them in Jesus name!

Love

Many of define Love as a feeling we have towards one another or a feeling we have towards someone. In fact, Love is just the opposite. Love is an action word that must be put into existence. We as women tend to use this word too loosely when it comes to men!

Let me explain. God showed his love for us by giving us his son Jesus (John 3:16). Not only did God say it, he put action behind it. Too many times we like to use this word Love when we know it's not coming from the heart. Do a self reflection, what are some of things or some of the people you put the word Love to?

Do you base your love off of an emotion or do you base your love off of the word of God?

One of the Ten Commandments says: Love your neighbor as thyself. This too is an action word (verb)

Many times in the bible when God tells us to do something, it deals with the heart which is our way of thinking, the core of us!

D A Y   1 3

◆ ◆ ◆

YOU ARE NOT damaged goods. No matter what pain has come upon you and you may barely be standing but you are still here. God is sustaining you. Some people may feel like you have nothing to be bothered by or it wasn't that bad but your pain is your pain. It may not seem like you have gone through anything to others but you fully well know about your sleepless nights and every tear that you have cried in secret.

Your heart has been broken, yes, but you are not a broken person. Sometimes it's absolutely necessary to step back and retreat from life and the people in it. It is imperative that you hear from and seek God at all times. Embrace your trials and when you don't understand, get before God and put a demand on Him to help you get understanding & wisdom about what it is you need to know at that moment.

Jesus loves you, you were not a mistake. (Jer. 1:5) God knows the plan that he has for you.

DAY 14

GOD IS ACCEPTING all flaws which includes; confusion, anger, depression, loneliness, drug/alcohol addition, lying etc... We can't overcome our sins without Jesus! He wants us to walk in him with boldness, happiness, peace, meekness, patience, long suffering, etc... Give Him your heart because everything abides there! Remember, today we are Ambassadors of Christ!!!

What are you holding back from Christ? He wants all of you good and bad, only in him will bad things change for the good.

Walk today in the newness of God. Every day brings brand new mercy and grace! Continue to stay in the right posture before him. Not only is man looking at us, but God is looking also. Today is the day that the Lord has made, let us rejoice and be glad in it. Make Godly choices today.

Are you walking in the fullness of the Lord? Does your praise in private reflect your praise in public?

D A Y   1 6

◆ ◆ ◆

BE KEEN TO the Holy Spirit today. Jesus left us the Holy Spirit to be a comforter and a guide. There are many things that the Lord wants to reveal to us, but we are too busy (doing nothing) to hear his voice. Our goal is to talk less and listen more, we will be surprised at what we here. It could be one word that will change our lives forever.

But the Comforter, *which is* the Holy Ghost, whom the Father will send in my name, he shall teach you all things, and bring all things to your remembrance, whatsoever I have said unto you. (John 14:26)

List some things that the Lord speaks to you in your quiet time.

D A Y   1 7

—— ◆ ◆ ◆ ——

I PRAY THAT your day is filled with Joy and peace. Allow God to rein over all of your decisions today. No problem is too hard for Him! So, if situations look impossible, just know that with God all things are possible to those that believe. (Mark 9:23)

Make a list of all the things and wants that you are believing God to provide. Start thanking him for his will in your life.

DAY 18

TODAY IS MAKE it happen Day! That thing you have been procrastinating to do, start pushing towards it. Whether it is writing a book, starting a business, working on self etc... It may be a simple smile today, make it happen! God is just waiting on you, He has already given you the power to succeed. Let's come against the power of procrastination!

What or who is stopping you from pushing forward?

D A Y 1 9

— ◆ ◆ ◆ —

STAND BOLD FOR the Lord today and do not waiver. Seek God in every decision that you make. Some of us believe for miraculous favor in certain situations being debt, health, marriage, children, job, etc... Whatever the situation is, Remember, in scripture..."But seek ye first the kingdom of God and His righteousness and all these things shall be added unto you'! God wants to be first in our lives! (Matthew 6:33)

What are you putting before God in your life? Make a list of it.

D A Y   2 0

— ◆ ◆ ◆ —

WHEN THE ENEMY tries to attack you with fear, anger, depression, loneliness, etc... Remember who your God is! Take a praise break today, think of all the things that God delivered you from or better yet kept you from. This is the day the Lord has made let us rejoice and be glad in it. (Psalm 118:4)KJV

Look back over your life and list all of the things that the Lord kept you from.

YOU ARE MORE THAN YOUR HAIR!

In today's society, we are looked at according to what our hair, clothes, shoes etc…looks like.

Being a hairstylist, I have seen a lot of women sit in and out of my chair. Sometimes, it amazes me on how much a women will put effort into her outer appearance. The longer these women sit in my chair; they began to reveal the hurt that lies beneath the outer shell of what we call Image. They will buy the most expensive hair to be weaved in, spending tons of money to make themselves feel better, only to witness that it is temporary. Week after week, I see the deep hurt that a lot of women endure. Whether it is a divorce, children, job or whatever the situation is, the common denominator is HURT.

While our appearance does matter, it should not define who we are as an individual. We define people according to social economic status instead of how God looks at us. This has caused a great alarm in our young girls today, many of our young girls are wearing extensions at an early age because that is how they see many of their looked upon T.V. idols. This has posed a challenge for the older generation to become champions for our young women. When I think of a champion, I think of someone who not only fight a battle and win, but someone who can stand in the gap for the younger generation as a bridge. We have to instill in our younger girls that they are special; they are Rubies, daughters of Zion. When I think of a Ruby, I think of a jewel. In fact, a Ruby is a special gem that was used by the High Kings in the biblical days. This special gem was used to light dark places. This is what our young girls are, or shall I say, our young women are. They are special gems that should give dark situations light. These gems must be handled with care.

Outer appearance does not fully cover up what is going on inside of us. Many of us are broken women who dress up the outside very well. We will buy expensive clothes, fashionable shoes, the best make-up to cover our flaws, but we are still hurting or damaged on the inside. God wants to touch the innermost being of our core which is the heart. We will try to run far away from our faults and fears. The only way that we can conquer our fears that have overtaken us as women, is to give in fully to Jesus Christ.

By having an intimate relationship with Jesus, we will begin to love ourselves as Jesus loves us. This is very vital to be who we are. To many times, we are looking for love in the wrong places. We are giving ourselves and our Spirits to be loved by someone who is capable of hurting us without even giving Jesus a chance. By seeing ourselves as God sees us, we will embrace our flaws and love ourselves no matter what our body looks like. We will demand respect because we respect ourselves, we will love one another because we love ourselves, and we will be who God says we are because we love Him!

D A Y   2 1

— ◆ ◆ ◆ —

GIVE GOD YOUR time this morning. Praying and believing that your day will be filled with Joy! Walk in Love today so that God will smile upon you, let your words be filled with anointing instead of condemnation. Remember, God looks at the heart of man in which man looks at works. Let our hearts remain pure before God.

But the LORD said unto Samuel, Look not on his countenance, or on the height of his stature; because I have refused him: for *the LORD seeth* not as man seeth; for man looketh on the outward appearance, but the LORD looketh on the heart. (1sam. 16:7) KJV

Are your words lining up with your walk?

D A Y   2 2

— ◆ ◆ ◆ —

Deut. 4:31 for the Lord your God is a merciful God; he will not abandon or destroy you or forget the covenant with your ancestors, which he confirmed to them by oath.

You have a covenant with God, the one that he swore to our ancestors: Abraham, Isaac and Jacob. This is a blood bought covenant that you have a right to. Exercise your right!

What is stopping you from exercising your right?

THINK ABOUT ALL of the things that you have to be thankful for. Let us put ourselves in a posture of thankfulness. Start to thank God just for who he is and not for what he does.

You have a lot to be thankful for, do some self-reflecting and allow yourself to be in a posture of praise.

D A Y   2 4

◆ ◆ ◆

REJOICE IN THE small things today. Step outside, breath in the morning dew, close your eyes, think of the goodness of the Lord. Smile, he protects those that belong to him. Stop worrying, he has never failed you before! Give all of your problems to him; he is in the business of making burdens light. All God is asking for is an obedient heart. I know you may say; "I sacrifice for people all the time". Remember, Jesus laid down (sacrificed) his life for ours because he obeyed the Father. The Bible says that obedience better than sacrifice, so God is not looking at your works, but your heart. Let us have a clean heart...

But Samuel replied, "What is more pleasing to the LORD: your burnt offerings and sacrifices or your obedience to his voice? Listen! Obedience is better than sacrifice, and submission is better than offering the fat of rams (1Sam.15:22)

Are you being obedient to what the Lord is saying? If not, list why.

YOUR POWER CAN influence for right or wrong, for victory or defeat. Speak words of encouragement today. Allow God's presence to flow through you freely to touch someone's life today. Remember, you can do what God called you to do. You do not have defeat in your bloodline because you have the blood of Jesus!

Are you using your power for Jesus? Or, are you using your power for the Enemy?

D A Y   2 6

◆ ◆ ◆

You were anointed for a purpose. Stop wasting what God equipped you with for the Enemy! Walking for God comes with a cost. It requires you to die to self every day. You can't live for God and the world at the same time. There will be some casualties of war during this walk. Just be sure to have your armor of God (Ephesians 6) on so that you won't become one of them! Walk in your anointing and don't apologize for it. Not everyone is going to like it, they didn't like Jesus either.

Have you surrendered your flesh to God? If not, what is holding you back?

D A Y　2 7

◆ ◆ ◆

SOMETHING THAT I am learning in life is to not sweat the small stuff literally! Every second, every minute cannot be recovered! Start smiling and laughing; you will truly start to see how small distractions are in your life. It's ok to veer off of your structured routine today to laugh at something that is funny. Don't be so uptight!

I dare you to smile at something today! I guarantee that you will enjoy it!

WHEN GOD BLESS you with a gift and a talent, you don't have to boast or puff yourself up for others. People will notice your humbleness, they may actually enjoy being around you!

Do a self check, do people enjoy being around you? If not, why?

D A Y   2 9

◆ ◆ ◆

MOVE FREELY IN Christ today. Anything that is chained and bound cannot move about freely. Many of us as Christians are just that! Chained and bound in our thought life. The Enemy knows that if we ever got the revelation of the Lord, we will be unstoppable. So, his job is to keep us in fear and disbelief. Continue to seek God and spend time with him so that he can break the chains off of you for good!

What have you bound? List them.

———— ◆ ◆ ◆ ————

KEEP YOUR MIND on Jesus. There, you will find perfect peace. Your job will not keep you in perfect peace, shopping will not keep you in perfect peace, women/men will not keep you in perfect peace. He will keep you in perfect peace, whose mind is stayed on him. (Isaiah 26:3)

What is taking you out of the perfect peace of God? Make a list...

D A Y   3 1

❖ ❖ ❖

IF YOU OPENED your eyes this morning God has given you another chance to get it right!

Make today just that, get it right! The only way to do that is to let Jesus reign over our lives in all of our decisions.

Does Jesus reign over your life?

D A Y   3 2

◆ ◆ ◆

THIS IS THE day the Lord has made I will rejoice and be glad in it, oh taste and see that the Lord is good and His mercy endures forever.

(Psalm 118:24)

What do you have to be thankful for? List them.

D A Y   3 3

◆ ◆ ◆

THROUGH HURT, PAIN, financial, brokenness etc... You can have all of the material things in the world, but if you don't have the peace of God on the inside, you're just faking happiness! There are a lot of us as women that do not have the peace of God on the inside so we turn to a temporary fix such as shopping etc... God wants to heal us from the inside out.

Are you running from God? Do you use temporary fixes for permanent solutions? If so, list them.

D A Y   3 4

◆ ◆ ◆

TODAY SEEK THE heart of God. God loves you even in your times of hurting and confusion, God loves you. Don't allow someone else to take control of your emotions, if you are a child of God, your mind, will and emotions belong to Him. Take time to look at yourself in the mirror and thank God for His creation which is YOU! Without the cover up, with your flaws, smile at yourself today. You were fearfully and wonderfully made!

I will praise thee; for I am fearfully *and* wonderfully made: marvelous *are* thy works; and *that* my soul knoweth right well. (Psalms 139:14)

Are you giving people or that someone power over your emotions?

D A Y 3 5

◆ ◆ ◆

IT FEELS GOOD when you can live life and laugh and it's not based off of material things. When you mature that's when and only when you will make mature decisions.

Is your life based off of material things? Take a moment to think about this.

D A Y   3 6

◆ ◆ ◆

SOMETIMES YOU HAVE to take a break from negative people, dream killers and word wasters!!!!

Who around you are killing your dreams? Take an inventory of your circle of friends.

D A Y   3 7

◆ ◆ ◆

GOD SAID THAT he will prepare a table in the presence of your enemies.....believe me, he will. When people are out to be you and want your life instead of theirs...believe that God has your back. The battle is the Lord's not yours! (Psalm 23:5)

God will do a much better job at taking care of your enemies than you can. Have you given your enemies over to him? Or, are you still trying to handle them yourself?

D A Y   3 8

Say: "I vow to go be me today"!

Live life to the fullest!   Expect favor and blessings today. "Nothing is impossible for me today". (Mark 11:23)

Have faith in God. This is vital, he is waiting on you.

Do you have faith that what you are seeking God for will come to past?

D A Y   3 9

◆ ◆ ◆

SAY: "SOMETHING GOOD is going to happen to me today. I walk in Authority and Dominion I will only speak words of positive power"!

Far above all rule and authority, power and dominion, and every title that can be given, not only in the present age but also in the one to come. (Ephesians. 1:21) NIV

◆ ◆ ◆

QUIT LETTING THE enemy come in your protective zone! You have to put up barriers that stop the enemy! Those barriers are the Word of God! (1peter5:8) tells us to be watchful... We have to be on the lookout!

Are you sober on the word of God? If not, why? What's stopping you?

It's Okay To Say No!

In life, there are many people that will drain most, if not all of your energy. We as women wear many hats in our lifetime. If we are not wearing the hat of mother, then we are wearing the hat of wife. If, we are not wearing the hat of wife, then we are wearing the hat of businesswoman or Taxi Driver! Sometimes, we stretch ourselves too thin. We will pile on and pile on responsibilities on top of responsibilities. The pile that we carry, most of the time is not even ours. We allow ourselves to take on other people problems that will cause weights in our lives. This begins to cause anxiety and stress in our lives that we don't need. We have to learn how to say NO! I know this is a very hard word to come out of our mouths. The funny thing is that we have no problem telling our kids and even our spouse No! But, when it comes to people we have a hard time saying this word. Life has to have balance with purpose. That's right, with purpose! Many of us are just coasting through life with no purpose. Let's define purpose; the reason in which something exist, done or made. You were designed with purpose and a calling. The sad thing is that many of us will never discover this in our lifetime. We will not allow our minds to become free from distraction and enablement. I know the word enablement is not a popular word to discuss, but let's discuss it. We enable people from obtaining their God given purpose because we want to rescue them from every situation that will help strengthen them. When we do things on purpose, then we should not be surprised with the results! If you say No, I can guarantee you that whatever it is, there will be a solution from somewhere else. Let's live life on purpose, and let's start by saying; I am created to live life with purpose and on purpose…It's starts with the word No!

◆ ◆ ◆

"LIVE LIFE ON purpose"! Due everything with excellence! After all, you were created with a purpose. God gave us instructions on how to live life, we just have to read the Manual.

If we were to play any type of sports, we would need to know what strategies to perform or what plays to run. We have to do that with the word of God, we must read to understand what God's will is for our life.

(Study to shew thyself approved unto God, a workman that needeth not to be ashamed, rightly dividing the word of truth. 2 Tim. 2:15) KJV

DAY 42

—— ◆ ◆ ◆ ——

TAKE A BREATHIER today; prioritize your list of things to do. Take time for yourself, it is needed. Even Jesus got to himself to think and pray. Don't always be surrounded by people and noise. The Holy Spirit is trying to speak to you and give you guidance. But, the only way to hear him is to have silence! Listen to the voice of wisdom.

(John 6:15) Jesus, knowing that they intended to come and make him king by force, withdrew again to a mountain by himself.

What has you so busy that you can't hear the voice of the Lord?

D A Y 4 4

◆ ◆ ◆

A WISE MAN will hear and increase in learning, and a man of understanding will acquire wise counsel.

(Proverbs 1:5) NASB

In order for us to hear, we must do less talking. In order for us to understand, we must surround ourselves with wise people. Look at your circle of friends; are they your wise counsel? Or, are they just wasting words?

D A Y   4 5

◆ ◆ ◆

BUT IF ANY of you lacks wisdom, let him ask of God, who gives to all generously and without reproach, and it will be given to him. (James 1:5)

God is waiting on you to ask for wisdom to do the impossible. While we are waiting on God, just know that God is waiting on us. Do not allow fear to cripple you, God gave you authority over fear in its entirety! Nothing of evil shall have dominion over you. You were created to have authority and to walk in wisdom to know the things of God. Looking at this verse, (James 1:5) it is very powerful. It shows how much God loves us and wants us to be whole in everything! He wants us to have the wisdom of him in order to overcome many tasks that we face today. It says that he gives generously without reproach. This means that he gives in large amounts without sorrow or regret…God is not in the business of taking back what he gives to us! He has so much more for us; we just have to be in a posture to receive.

Are you in a posture to receive the blessings of God?

By understanding his word, a clean heart and a willing spirit. I think you are!

91

Made in the USA
Monee, IL
07 July 2026

56551497R00059